A Poor Man's Guide
to Building Wealth
with Precious Metals

Greg Robards

ISBN:1512333212
ISBN-13:9781512333213

DEDICATION

To the love of my life Deb

CONTENTS

ACKNOWLEDGMENTS

I would like to thank all of the authors who have shared their insights with me over the years, and to the commentators of television and radio who helped me to make sense out of personal finances. Most of all, I want to thank my Lord and Savior Jesus Christ who brings real value and worth to my life.

Why This Book Is Important

As I write this booklet, there is great uncertainty in the economies of the United States and the world. Journalism has become more subjective than factual. Reports issued by the government on the economic state of the Union are colored by political agendas. The national debt rises logarithmically. The Federal Reserve prints money as fast as the government can spend it, without it being tied to any tangible assets. The current administration inflates numbers, and then rounds almost every economic report down, after the first release of data, in order to give the impression of financial stability and growth.

The United States of America is not the only country to employ these practices. Unlike earlier periods in our history, the economies of the world are linked together, and dependent upon one another, so that any downturn in one part of the world becomes a drain on all. World leaders use the power of their economies to exert influence on other countries. Economists representing individual countries are continually exploring venues to gain an advantage over others. Cyber-thieves threaten individual, as well as national wealth. The world economy is a like a house of cards, which could be blown down overnight, as world events change. What can the average person do to protect himself or herself in case of economic collapse?

Those who control vast sums of money understand how the system works. They have the resources to protect themselves, and to make money, regardless of the state of the economy. Many, who are in the middle and lower economic brackets, feel that there is nothing they can do to prepare for an economic downturn, much less build financial wealth. Many live in a simple state of faith that everything will work out, and they will deal with whatever comes, when they have to. I also am a man of faith, but I understand that I have to take some personal responsibility, and practice discipline, if I want to be prepared, and to get ahead financially.

Many years ago my wife and I lived from paycheck to paycheck. We were in debt, and without a sense of financial security. Today we are not wealthy people, by the world's standards, but we have accumulated some wealth, that we would never have had, without putting into practice some sound financial principles.

Investment is the key to financial security. Anyone who wants to build wealth must invest. While there are many investments, and each person must determine which vehicle is best for them, the focus of this book is investing in precious metals. It is aimed at the individual who thinks that they do not have any money to invest, and to the person who wants to learn more about investing in the precious metals market.

What I will share with you, in the pages of this book, are principles that I have learned from books, articles on the Internet, and, most of all, practical suggestions that come from personal experience. It is my prayer that every reader will gain valuable insight that will help him or her with their financial decisions and goals, and will allow them to build personal wealth, by investing in precious metals, over time.

Build Wealth Without Spending Any More Money

The reason why most people do not save, or invest, is that they have been conditioned to believe that they do not have any extra money. They have too many bills, or too many obligations. One unexpected thing after another produces a financial drain. Creditors hound them, and they have to ask for extensions on their loans. Sometimes they find a solution by refinancing their homes, or selling purchased items at a loss. While these actions may be necessary in certain situations, overall it reveals a symptom of a lack of the discipline needed for financial responsibility.

Within the culture of the United States, people are brainwashed to believe that they must possess every new item that is introduced on the consumer market. Often people are unwilling to save up for their purchase, so they use credit cards, or high interest financing, in order to have whatever it is they want, when they want it. There are some items that the average person must pay for by installment. Most people cannot pay cash for their home, or their car. Other items wind up costing far more than he or she would be willing to pay, if they took into account the accumulated finance and interest charges, before they made the purchase.

Most of these wealth-draining purchases are based upon impulse buying. If a person desires a new $600 cell phone, rather than pulling out the credit card, he or she would be better served with the mind-set to save up the money, and pay cash. Paying cash makes it harder to spend money, because the money passes through a person's hands in real time. When a person pays cash, he or she thinks about the possible better uses for their money. The buyer sees the money going away with the purchase. Paying with cash means that you will not give somebody else your money, just so that you can have that item in your possession earlier than if you had to save for it. The discipline of paying cash also helps to eliminate the power of impulse buying. As time passes, the buyer may decide that he or she really doesn't need a new cell phone at all, and will save that money to use somewhere else, or to invest. A good friend of mine says that on any major purpose, a person should give themselves three days and a wake up, so that they have time to think through their purchase, and determine whether or not they should buy it. These practices are wonderful tools to help people keep from accumulating unrealistic debt.

I know that the problem faced by some of the people who read this book will be that they are already sinking in debt, and see no way to climb out. A large percentage of their income goes to paying the interest on their loans, and credit cards. They make the minimum payments on each account in order to stretch their dollars. They live payday-to-payday, trying to pay their bills, but they never get caught up, much less get ahead. High interest debt is modern day slavery for people caught in its grasp.

There was a point in my life when I was trapped in debt. Nothing in my situation would have changed, had I not made it my goal to get out of debt. I will concede that my life's situation changed in large measure because of the influence my faith made in my life, and God's direct hand of blessing, but I also realized that I bore personal responsibility for the way that I handled my finances.

Because of personal debt, my credit score was low. With a low credit score, every loan, credit card, and finance contract, carried a high interest rate. Here is a truth to consider: people, who can afford it the least, pay the highest interest rate on everything. Others, who have a track record of financial responsibility, secure a lower interest rate on all of their credit purchases, thus they are in a better position to build financial security.

Get out of debt. Penalties for late payments are the highest form of interest, so pay every bill on time, every time. Always try to pay more than the minimum due, so that you shorten the longevity of your debt. Make a plan to pay off your loans with the highest interest rates first. Only pay the minimum amount due if it will allow you to pay off another bill in that month. When you pay off a bill, take the amount of that monthly payment, and apply it to the next highest interest loan, in addition to the payment you are already making. Continue this process until you climb out of the financial hole. Eliminating debt frees up money for investment, but it requires self-discipline. Don't take on any unnecessary debt until you are certain you can afford to pay it back, without compromising your financial plan, and consistently pay yourself through investments.

Once you pay off a loan, do not close out the account. In this way you have an established line of credit that will have a positive influence on your credit score. If you have high interest credit cards that you have paid off, don't use them, or use them sparingly, and pay them off, in full, at the end of the month, to avoid any interest charges. Soon, low interest credit card offers will come in the mail, some with six month, one year, or eighteen month interest-free offers. Do not use them frivolously, but use them wisely to make larger purchases, without having to pay any interest. Do not use them unless you are certain that you can pay them off before the expiration of the offer.

Some credit cards offer lower interest than others. Some

have longer grace periods, which allows a person to extend the amount of time they have to pay. Always pay the balance off before the due date. By using credit cards wisely, and responsibly, a person can increase their credit score, secure lower interest rate loans, and expand their buying power, even if they are not making any more money. By climbing out of debt, money saved on finance charges, late fees, and interest, are freed up for investment. This is an essential strategy for building wealth.

By living debt free, or near debt free, much stress will be relieved, which will help to lead to a happier, and more productive life. Without the stress of debt, a person is able to think more clearly, and responsibly, about their finances, and enjoy a happier life. This takes ongoing discipline, but the rewards far exceed the temporary pleasure that might come with purchases made that incur irresponsible debt. These are tangible plans to enable a person to begin to build financial security.

People discover other places to find money for investment, by honestly asking if there are things they buy, which are frivolous, or unnecessary, for them to have a quality lifestyle. One of the greatest areas of financial drain comes from addictions, to which people succumb, that not only exhausts their finances, but also, in time, degrade the quality of their lives.

I have read that people in the United States who make less than $20,000 per year spend, on average, 9% of their total income on lottery tickets. In Florida, when the state lottery was first approved, it seemed like everyone bought tickets. Economic status did not matter, because it was new, and exciting to the people who played. As soon as the new wore off, and people realized the odds against winning, most of those who were financially secure stopped buying tickets. The people who could least afford it, however, began buying in greater quantities.

A person, who works hard and makes $20,000 a year, on

average, spends $1800 per year in lottery tickets. Most, who do win a small amount on scratch off tickets, spend their winnings on more chances. At the end of the year they have nothing to show for their $1800 investment. If they had taken that same money, using prices at the time of this writing, they could have purchased an ounce and a half of gold, or a hundred ounces of silver. Over five years they could have $9,000 in investment savings, plus the interest accrued.

The lotteries across our country are big business, and they are the most severe of all taxes upon the poor. The lottery appeals to desperation, and the hope of a quick fix to financial struggles. All gambling is rigged in the house's favor, and the odds at winning at the lottery are the worst. Why is it that you will hardly ever see a wealthy person standing in line to buy lottery tickets? It is because they refuse to throw their money away. If a person is playing the lottery, they have money that could be applied toward investments and building wealth.

According to a recent survey, a person who smokes cigarettes, at the rate of a pack a day, will spend anywhere from $1,916 to $4,690 a year, depending upon where they live. As an ex-smoker myself, I know all the arguments a person might give for continuing to smoke. If a person wants to smoke, that is his or her business. At the end of the year, what does a smoker have to show for their expenditure: poor health, increased medical expenses? What might happen if they kicked the habit? By redirecting those funds to savings, they could have a substantial start in the wealth building process, and improve their health, while extending their life expectancy. Health insurance premiums would go down, and they could enjoy an overall improved quality of their life.

A 2012 study showed that the average American spends 1% of their income on alcohol. According to this statistic, the average person making $50,000 per year spends $500 on alcohol. While that does not seem like a lot of money to some people, at current prices, that person could buy a roll of twenty, one-ounce silver coins, with money left over. The statistic is misleading, because the average includes people who do not drink. People, who drink on a regular basis, or habitually, spend a much higher percentage of their income. Those who drink at bars, or clubs, spend more than those who drink at home. When people are under the influence of alcohol, they tend to be less careful about other expenses they might incur. This does not take into account unexpected legal fees, or medical expenses, that might come as a result of long term addiction, or actions taken by authorities, while a person is under the influence.

A six-pack of beer averages about $5. In some places it is much higher. Premium beers cost even more. Using the lower $5 figure, if a person drinks a six-pack per week, they will spend $260 a year that could have been used to build wealth. The argument for drinking is that people are just social drinkers, they like a glass of wine with their meals, or they need alcohol to unwind. Each individual has the right to choose whether or not to drink. If, however, someone is unwilling to at least consider the option of using money spent on alcohol for some other use, he or she may have a problem of addiction, and are probably spending far more than $260 per year.

The same point may be made of people who use recreational drugs. In 2014, the Chicago Tribune reported on the average price of marijuana by state. Their findings concluded that an ounce of high quality marijuana costs anywhere from $200 to $350, or more per ounce, on the street. The price of medical marijuana is expected to settle somewhat higher. Other drugs carry a similar cost. These figures do not take into account the lack of productivity, slower response times that can contribute to accidents, missed workdays, and the compromise to a person's ability to reason, which drug abuse produces. There is no way to accurately calculate how drug abuse might affect a person's lifetime income, from lack of advancement, or the cost of an encounter with the legal system.

The point is not to condemn anyone who engages in these activities, but to help people to understand how lifestyle choices play a major role in their ability to build wealth. If a person who has two or more of these addictive tendencies were able to free themselves from them, they would be amazed at how much more money they would have to work with.

Other suggestions for saving money include, not wasting food, or throwing away leftovers. Shop for a trustworthy bank that waves excessive fees. Be careful about third party ATM fees. Follow your power company's recommendations for saving energy. Don't shop at convince stores, and gas stations, for items you can purchase just down the street at a lesser price. Allow yourself to purchase generic brands. Grow some of your own food. Don't be too lazy to return items. Be careful about how often you eat out. Consider cutting the coax from your Cable Company, or Satellite Television Provider. Shop for the best loans and credit cards. Don't buy new things you don't need. Don't pay someone else to do things you can do yourself. Look carefully for a good used car before you buy a new one. Don't acquire an impossible college debt, which you will never be able to pay off. Take care of your health, so that you don't have unnecessary medical costs. Plan your purchases, so that you do not have to make unnecessary trips to the store.

Another source of revenue worth consideration for investment is what I call windfalls. Windfalls are funds a person receives, which are not a part of their normal monthly income. Rather than blowing an Income Tax Return on unnecessary items, use that money to invest. Mortgage companies are required to refund overpayments on escrow accounts. Other refunds, gifts, or earnings that come to a person, over and above their monthly cash flow, are funds, which could be used for investment.

This is just a partial list to get the reader's creative juices flowing. People tend to do whatever they really want to do. If a person wants to create, and grow personal wealth, they have to let that goal influence their decision making process. Almost everyone can find ways to stretch their dollars, and free up income for investment, if they want to. The challenge is to find those areas where he or she wastes money, and turn those dollars into assets.

There are two other tools, which have helped me personally, to have more money to invest. The first is that I save all of my change at the end of the day. If I spend $1.49, $.51 goes into a jar, a box, or a tin, and sits there until it is overflowing. If I spend $1.01, I save $.99. Over time, that money accumulates. A couple of years ago I ran across a silver product I wanted to add to my holdings, but I did not have enough money to make the investment. I took all of the accumulated change to the bank, cashed it in, and had more than I needed. This is an easy tool to use that helps the investor learn how to save. The more change you add to your holdings, the more it grows, and the easier it is to see how investing over time builds wealth.

Another practice that I have found beneficial is rounding up my purchases in my checkbook. Every time I write a check, pay online through Billpay, or use a debit card, I enter the exact figure into my check register, but round that figure up when calculating the balance. When I balance the checkbook, I confirm that all of the checks have cleared, and the funds have flowed in and out as they should, but I leave the surplus in the checking account.

By doing this I have hundreds of dollars in reserve for

emergencies, without experiencing any sacrifice for saving that money. If I need to take the balance recorded in my checkbook below zero occasionally, the money is there in reserve. With the next deposit, I replace whatever appears as a negative balance, and the money continues to grow over time.

If the reader considers these principles, he or she will be able to come up with other ideas to save money, and to see that almost everyone has money to invest, when they discipline themselves, and handle their finances responsibly.

Why Precious Metals?

Precious metals may not be the best investment, and certainly, for most people, should not be their only investment. Anyone who works for a company who offers to contribute to their retirement plan should take full advantage. If the employer matches the employee's contribution, the employee should have the maximum amount taken out of their paycheck each pay period, in order to get the maximum matching funds. Don't think that you cannot afford it. You will adjust, because everyone tends to spend, and to make do with, whatever he or she has. Think instead about how you are going to get a higher return on your investment, than with any other investment opportunity.

Say for example, your employer will match your contribution, dollar for dollar, up to $100, in their retirement program. Under those conditions, you should put the full $100 into your retirement account every payday. Each pay period, you will have a 100% return on your investment, instantly. Instead of saving $100, you will realize $200. The compound interest earned over time on this investment will be the quickest, and most efficient, way to build wealth. These programs also give the employee a tax break, which, for most people, will be like investing an additional 15% to 20% over what money they would otherwise have had available to invest, if they had to pay taxes up front. If a person's retirement savings are heavily invested in stocks, and the stock market drops 50% overnight, he or she hasn't lost any of their original investment. In fact, that person still will have gained half of the interest accumulated on the full amount that has been placed into the account over time.

When stocks fall, don't panic. Take a long view on your investments. Historically the market has always recovered, and people, who stay in during the lean times, and continue to invest, make the most money. Whenever the stock market falls, I see it as an opportunity to increase my shares at a bargain price. I enjoy watching the recovery, because I know my long-term investment is making money for me.

This may not be true for the person who plans to work for a company for only a short period of time, or for a plan that may have uncertain, or mismanaged investment policies. Some companies require that a person work for them a number of years before they are fully vested. Do your research, and determine if their plan will work for you. In most circumstances, it will be hard to find a better return on your investment.

When I first started putting financial strategies to work, I did not invest in precious metals, but rather I put my savings into Certificates of Deposit. CDs are a low risk investment. An investor enters into a contractual agreement that will deliver a fixed interest on the investment, no matter what happens in the economy. The interest return rate on a CD is lower than the potential return of most other investments, and it is tied to the prime interest rate. When interest rates are high, so are the returns on CDs. I chose CDs to help me to discipline myself to save. I put money into my savings account until I had enough to purchase a CD. I would not consider cashing in a CD until it had matured, and I had made some money off the investment. After buying one, I repeated the process and acquired more over time.

As the economy fell, and the Federal Reserve lowered interest rates, buying CDs became no more profitable than sticking money in a mattress. When allowing for inflation, CDs and savings accounts were loosing money, over time. As my CDs matured, I cashed them in, and began investing in precious metals. If interest rates climb, and the spot price of precious metals becomes over inflated, I may choose to purchase CDs instead of buying more metal, but I will hold on to the gold and silver I have already purchased, and reinvest the matured CD money, when the price of precious metals falls to a reasonable level.

For the big investors, precious metals are commodities to be traded on the Exchange. Vast fortunes change hands every day. Some people invest in stocks that fund the mines, or the processors who produce the finished product. For the average person, these kinds of investments are speculative, risky, and out of reach.

The attractive aspect of precious metals investment is that a person purchases a product that holds its core value. An investor can hold it in his or her hand, and keep it in their possession. Most other investments are on paper, and are tied to the value of paper dollars. If the value of the dollar falls, the purchasing power of precious metals remains somewhat constant, or it increases over time.

Buying precious metals, for the average person, should be considered a long-term investment. There are proprietors of coin shops, and bullion dealers, who exchange precious metals for a living, but that is beyond the reach of most people, and beyond the scope of this book. Many people use e-bay, or web pages, to set up virtual stores, to sell their holdings. This may be an option for some reading this book, but my observation is that most sellers spend too much time, and work too hard, at making very little money this way.

The strategies in this book are not offered as a get rich quick scheme, but as a workable plan, for people of modest means, to build wealth over time. At the time of this writing, the interest paid in savings accounts and annuities cannot keep up with the rate of inflation. Bonds generally tie up people's money for longer periods of time, and produce less profit than other investments.

Costs associated with purchasing stocks, and the volatility of the markets, makes them very risky investments for people who do not have a lot of money to invest. Precious metals are much more attractive, in that a person may invest less than $20, at the time of this writing, and have in their possession an ounce of silver. If that same person commits to investing a similar amount each week, they will accumulate 52 ounces of silver in one year. The value of silver will rise and fall, but the investor maintains, and possesses his or her real assets, regardless of what happens to investments tied to paper.

Consider the currency of the United States. All currency was once tied to gold and silver. The Federal Government guaranteed that they would exchange paper dollars for an equivalent value of precious metal. Gold and silver have been used to establish the value of purchased items since the beginning of recorded history. Dollars tied to gold and silver gave people confidence in the value of their currency. It kept the government honest, and the people used their money with confidence in its value.

When dollars changed to Federal Reserve Notes, people had to trust that the Federal Reserve, and the government, would back the dollar's value. The only real asset the Federal Reserve has to offer is their ability to print more dollars. Our economy today is a system built upon printed paper, backed by the promise of more printed paper. We use dollars because we need them for commerce, but confidence in the staying power of the dollar wanes in light of the ever-growing accumulated debt, into trillions of dollars.

Real value is not measured in dollars, but in purchasing power. When dollars reach the point that their value is little more than the paper they are printed on, precious metals will maintain their purchasing power. In a totally failed economic situation, where inflation causes dollars to loose nearly all their value, precious metals will become the preferred standard of exchange, and their purchasing power will skyrocket.

Traditionally, experts have claimed that precious metals' value changed inversely proportional to the stock market. If stocks went up, precious metals value would fall. If stocks were down, precious metals value would rise. This was an observable phenomenon analysts could plot over the years. At the time of this writing, the economy is erratic, and this general rule of thumb does not hold true the way economists have come to predict. The stock market is driven more by emotion, than true economic indicators. Investors are afraid, because the stock market has been propped up with paper, more than with tangible assets. A rumor can send the stock market in a downward spiral, whether there is any truth in it or not. Current events cause knee-jerk reactions. People are afraid of the national debt, and the ever-higher ceiling of debt that is necessary to just keep the economy moving. The news media reports instantly on the ever-changing, and unstable, world situation. Investors are faced with the very real possibility that they could loose all of their money, and one tragic event could wipe out all of their investments.

To understand what the true effects of this fear on the precious metals market, the investor must take a long view. We have day-traders who seek to profit on erratic swings in the markets. People stay glued to the moment-by-moment reports, as they come over the wire. Everyone is trying to profit from every rise and fall. No wonder the markets are so erratic, and unstable.

If an investor studies the charts of stocks and precious metals, over a period of decades, rather than days, or hours, they can see the trends more as waves, rather than saw teeth or lightning bolts. The investor can observe that the inverse relationship between stocks and precious metals still exists, but they cannot be seen in the microcosm of day-to-day or moment-to-moment trading. What can also be seen is the fact that the overall value of precious metals is increasing, because of the fear of investors in other markets.

The investor in precious metals can take advantage of this knowledge by watching the markets, and timing their purchases. The emotional feelings of Wall Street that the economy is getting better, causes stocks to begin to climb higher. The precious metals market seems to lag slightly, but in time the improved market will force precious metal values to fall. Likewise, if the trend over several days, weeks, or months shows a fall in the stock market, metal's prices will rise, as more people move their money to invest in gold and silver. This cycle, based upon supply and demand, repeats itself over and over, not in real time, but over extended time.

See Spot Run

A good plan for building wealth is to buy a little gold or silver as you go, regardless of the market price. Consider buying a roll of 90% silver coins, or a few ounces of silver bullion every pay-period, or every month. I have used this strategy and bought precious metals when the spot price was higher than it is at present, and when it was lower. If I think only in terms of todays price, I have paid too much for some of the metal that I have purchased, and I got a real bargain on other purchases. The flip side is that if I had not been buying all along, I would not have accumulated any wealth. This method of planning purchases balances out the fluctuations in the market, and is a consistent means of increasing one's holdings.

Once a person accumulates a quantity of precious metals, they may want to hold their investment dollars for the most opportune time to buy. The best time to purchase precious metals is when the spot price is at its lowest. The spot price may be defined as the dollar value placed upon a commodity, which may change from moment to moment, while the markets are open. Small investors do not buy directly from the markets, but from dealers, brokers, or individuals who offer the product for sale. Some bullion dealers change their sale price to the public in real time, as they follow the rise and fall on the exchange. Spot is an indicator that drives the cost to the consumer. On the market there is a price that someone is willing to offer, and a price at which someone is willing to sell. For the dealer, the sell price marks the value of the metal, and a premium is added to the consumer. Spot + premium = cost to consumer. The cost to the investor is generally more than spot. If you stumble on an opportunity to buy at, or below spot, buy all that you can afford.

As I write this chapter, over the last six months, the spot price of silver has reached as high as $18.31 per ounce. The lowest spot price fell to $15.96. For me, and for now, my buy price is $16.00 per ounce. The erratic swings in the silver market are ongoing, but eight times, in the last six months, spot prices have fallen to below $16.00. I purchased some silver at the last dip, and I am sitting on my investment dollars, as I wait for the next dip. Why not save a couple of dollars an ounce if you can? Of course there is no guarantee that the spot price will fall to that level again in the near future, or at all, but the trends are there.

The beauty of owning precious metals is that they always maintain a core value. An investor in stocks stands to make great gains, because they are taking a great risk: the more aggressive the stock, the greater the risk. Risk means that the investor could loose a portion, or all, of their investment. There are risks involved for the precious metals investor as well, but little or no risk of the commodity loosing all of its value. These metals are somewhat rare. While they are still mined today, there is not an unlimited supply. There is a real demand for industrial, as well as investment, use. Supply and demand makes metals an attractive alternative, or supplement, to stocks. An investor might loose money on his or her investment, but they will never loose it all. Metals are a safer, and a more stable investment, than many other options.

This also helps to explain why an investor should consider precious metals as a long-term investment. Don't try to make a quick killing by buying metals, and then immediately selling them at a profit, unless you are trying to make this your career. The purpose of this book is to show how the average person can build wealth over time, not how to get rich quick.

There is another fear that currently drives the precious metals market. This is the fear that world economies, and global relationships, are so unstable, that there is a real possibility of a total economic collapse. This scenario could arise from many quarters. If a person believes that this is a legitimate possibility, having at least some precious metals might make the difference between perishing and survival.

Some years back, after a hurricane on the gulf coast, all of the banks were closed, and only a few businesses were able to open. I read a story of a man who went to a gas station, and offered a Silver Eagle in exchange for some fuel. The attendant was happy to accept the coin, because he recognized the value of an ounce of silver. In a prolonged disaster situation, or a total collapse of the economy, precious metals will likely become the preferred method of exchange. If it gets even worse, it won't matter anyway. Let's pray for the best, and continue to build wealth for our children, as well as ourselves, as we hope for brighter days ahead.

The spot price of precious metals is in a constant state of flux. A simple web search will reveal real-time spot prices, as well as historical performance. It is an indicator of the value of a commodity in relationship to other investment opportunities. The spot price is influenced by all the factors in the economy. Take advantage of lower prices when you can, but do not let your focus on the spot price keep you from building wealth.

Buy Low, Don't Sell

Regardless of the spot price, the investor in precious metals needs to carefully consider where to make their purchases. People with more money than time often choose a bullion broker to help them with all of their purchases. They generally pay a little extra for the service and convenience a broker provides. Not all brokers are the same, and I encourage anyone reading this book to consider using their services. You might find one who will be able to offer precious metals to you at a lower price than you can find elsewhere.

There are other options that may yield a lower price on your purchases. Almost every small town has at least one or two coin shops. I do not buy from coin shops very often, but I have stumbled across some good deals from time to time. By all means, visit the local coin and bullion dealers in your area. Even if you don't find a really great deal, buy something from them, at a reasonable price, to help you to establish a relationship with them. A good coin dealer may be able to give you advice and insight into the market, and they may be able to lead you to a great buy, depending upon what you are looking for.

Almost every flea market has someone who keeps a table where they sell coins and supplies. If you are at a flea market anyway, stop by and see what they have. My experience has been that I can almost always find a better source, but from time to time you may get lucky.

There has been a lot written about checking your change for 90% silver coins. I have done this for many years, and can spot a silver coin at a glance. By the same token, it has been many years since I have actually found a silver coin this way. Some books recommend that you establish a relationship with a bank employee, or a convenience store clerk, and pay them for whatever silver they find and save for you. You can find opportunities on ebay to buy unchecked half dollar rolls that may have some silver coins: maybe, but not likely. I have tried it myself and found nothing. The truth is that the US government stopped minting 90% silver coins in 1964. People have been checking their change for over fifty years, so it is very unlikely that you will find much silver in everyday circulation. Do check your change anyway, it only takes a second, and you never know when someone's grandchild might have dipped their hands into Grandma's stash to buy a soda, or an ice cream cone, not knowing that they are spending silver coins.

My personal preference is to buy online. By buying online, the investor is able to maintain some anonymity. It may be unwise to let the general public think that you have a hoard of silver or gold in your home. The biggest reason I buy online is that I can find what I want at a consistently lower price, than what I have been able to find locally. One of the biggest concerns that I had was, that by buying online, someone might rip me off. That has never happened. I have always received what I ordered. If I wasn't totally satisfied with my order, it has always been my fault for not reading the full description carefully.

I deal with multiple vendors to find the lowest price on the item I want to buy. When companies compete for business, the consumer always comes out ahead. When you compare prices, be careful to check for shipping charges, sales tax, or broker fees. These unseen costs quickly turn what appears to be a bargain into a poor investment.

Radio, TV, and social media sites often advertise companies that sell gold and silver. Check them out, but in every case, so far, I have been able to purchase like products at a lower price from other sources. I do not have any affiliation with these two sources, other than I am a customer. Whenever I purchase bullion, I always check online with JM Bullion at www.jmbullion.com, and APMEX at www.apmex.com. These two vendors consistently offer lower prices than other bullion dealers. Periodically I check with other sellers, but for some time now, these two have proven to offer the lowest prices on precious metals, when the purchaser pays cash. I keep a file on my computer, with multiple websites, so that I can quickly compare prices.

Plan to pay cash, because the best bullion dealers sell close to the margin, and must make up the expense incurred by consumers using credit cards. If a person buys on credit, and he or she does not pay their bill, in full, by the end of the month, with the added interest charges, they will pay too much. Most online companies will post two different prices: one for cash (paper check), the other for credit. An investor always saves money with cash.

Purchasing items online requires patience. Bullion dealers wait at least five days after they receive your check, before processing your order, in order to give time for your check to clear. Credit card orders process more quickly, but at a higher cost. Most people want the product in their hand as soon as possible, but it can take two or three weeks sometimes to receive an order. That is really not an issue when making a long-term investment. The order will come, and the investor has locked in the price, before the market could change.

Another source worth considering is ebay. Is ebay a good place to buy precious metals? The answer is yes, no, maybe, sometimes, or almost never, depending on what you want to buy, and how much time you want to spend buying it. If you look at the "buy it now" prices on ebay, and compare them to that of the bullion dealers, almost always the dealers sell the same product for less. Many bullion dealers also sell on ebay, and they may have certain items on sale. Recently APMEX has posted offerings on ebay at prices lower than what they advertised in their online stores, so it still pays to check ebay.

A few weekends ago I ran a test. I checked APMEX for their price on a roll of 90% silver US coins, because at that time, their rolls sold for less than other vendors. I went to ebay and bid on 36 different auctions for rolls of 90% silver coins. In some of those auctions I bid the exact price that I could buy it from APMEX, became the highest bidder, and waited until after the auction closed to check the results. Other auctions, I waited until the end of the auction to place my bid, and limited my final bid to the APMEX price. In all 36 instances, I could buy the rolls from APMEX, cheaper than I could have bought them on ebay.

With many other silver and gold products, JM Bullion offers the best price. Generally, ebay becomes the place to buy when a person wants to add to their holdings, items not offered by the bullion companies. We will explore these possibilities in the chapters that follow.

Conventional wisdom is to buy low and sell high. In order to build wealth, buy low, and don't sell at all. Money in a checking account has a way of being used up. If there is something you want, or someplace you want to go. If you have the money in your checking account, it is too easy to spend it on items that have no lasting value. I am not saying that an investor should never go out to eat, or to have fun. Everyone needs these kinds of activities in order to live a healthy and well-adjusted life. In balance, we all have to discipline ourselves against wasting money, if we hope to build wealth.

Liquid assets resting in checking accounts are easy to spend. Money, kept in a savings account, is too easy to transfer into checking, or to dip into at the local ATM. Money invested in precious metals has to be sold before it can be converted into cash. That extra step makes it harder to spend, which is a blessing to the person wanting to build wealth. If a person treats their holdings as liquid assets, and is constantly buying and then selling, they are going to loose money in the long run, and not have anything to show for it. Might as well go back to the bad habits that kept them broke in the past.

The purpose of this book is to offer a solid plan for having and keeping precious metal investments. This is the only way anyone can build personal wealth, over time, but you have to know what to buy.

An Ounce, Is an Ounce, Is an Ounce, Unless It's a Troy Ounce

We use the term "ounces" as a unit of measure for weight, or volume. That soda you bought came in a twelve, sixteen, or twenty-ounce bottle. Your recipe requires four ounces of ground beef. Since there are sixteen ounces in a pound, you know to cut off a quarter pound to put in the skillet.

The mass of precious metals is measured in an empirical unit called the troy ounce. Other products are measured in the more common avoirdupois ounces. The definition of a troy ounce is that it is exactly .0311034768 kilograms, or 31.1034768 grams. This means that a troy ounce has 1.09714 times more mass than an avoirdupois ounce. Just in case you are not already confused enough; there are twelve troy ounces in a troy pound, and 14.5833 troy ounces in an avoirdupois pound.

If the spot value of silver is $17 per ounce, it refers to a troy ounce. If you see an auction on ebay for an ounce, or a pound, of common silver coins, they are probably talking about avoirdupois ounces and pounds, and 90% silver. If you bid $17, and thinking you are getting an ounce of silver at spot, you are not. All precious metals are measured in troy ounces. Make sure you are getting what you think you are buying.

The exception is that bullion is sometimes sold in grams or kilograms. One avoirdupois ounce contains 28.3495231 grams, but precious metals are measured with troy ounces, which contain 31.1034768 grams. In most transactions you will not need to worry about these conversions, but you must be aware of the differences in measurement, so that some unscrupulous seller doesn't rip you off.

Another important consideration in purchasing precious

metals is that a coin's value changes with its condition. A coin that is heavily worn or damaged might have little or no value over its silver or gold content. That same coin in uncirculated condition could be worth thousands of dollars. Coins are generally graded by what is called the Sheldon Scale, named after its inventor William Sheldon. The scale goes from one through seventy, one being a totally slick coin, and seventy being a perfect coin. The scale is broken down into sections, and the ones you will be most interested in are as follows: AG = almost good Ag-3), G= good (G4-6), VG = very good (VG8-10), F = fine (F12-15), VF = very fine (VF20-35), EF = extra fine (EF40-45), AU = about uncirculated (AU50-58), and MS or PF = mint state and proof (MS/PF60-70). BU (brilliant uncirculated) refers to a MS (mint state) coin with a lustrous finish. PF refers to coins that are specially minted with the collector in mind. They are harder, and more expensive, to produce, and carry an additional initial premium over MS coins. Sometimes these values will be followed with a plus sign to show that they are nearly at the next highest grade.

Grading coins is a subjective process, but the difference in value between a VF coin and an EF coin could be in the hundreds or thousands of dollars. You might purchase a coin that is described as an AU, but when you receive your purchase, you might rate it at MS, or EF. Who is to say for sure?

To eliminate ambiguity, people sometimes pay to have their coins professionally graded, and thus to establish their true value. After being graded, these coins are placed in a plastic protector called a slab, and marked with the determined grade. The problem is that grading remains subjective, and not all grading services are equal. Especially on ebay, you will run into coins from many different grading services. In some cases, the seller, or company, that has them up for auction, will have produced these slabs themselves. As far as re-sell value is concerned, these slabs serve only as a protective cover, and buyers will not, or should not, accept them automatically at the advertised grade.

There are two grading services that are nearly universally accepted by buyers and investors. PCGS stand for Professional Coin Grading Service. They are considered to be the strictest and best in terms of accurately grading coins, and the preferred company by many. NGC stands for Numismatic Guaranty Corporation, and they come in at a very close second, as far as acceptance for reliable grading. Nearly all collectors and dealers will accept the grade, and honor the worth, of a coin that has been graded by either of these services. Other companies do a good job of grading as well, and the buyer may be able to find a real bargain on a coin in one of their slabs. As an investor, you must weigh these things, because it will have an effect on any future return.

In spite of what I have said above, I have on occasion, purchased silver dollars and other rare coins, slabbed by unknown graders, and even known graders with a bad track record. Even when the grade did not live up to its claim, I still received a huge discount over what I would have paid for that same coin had it been accurately graded by one of the premiere companies. Buyer beware, it is up to the individual to determine the condition, and value, of the coin they are about to purchase. When purchasing coins that far exceed the value of their metal content, do your research before you buy.

For the most part I have been referring to older collectable coins. In recent years, however, there has been a massive movement to have modern coins, and bullion coins, graded. Modern bullion coins have become extremely collectable, and a perfect, graded, MS70 of PF70 coin, slabbed by a reputable service, carries a much higher premium than a lower grade or ungraded coin.

Which Precious Metals Do I Buy?

Speculators in precious metals invest in platinum, palladium, gold, silver, and copper. At the time of this writing, the spot price for one troy ounce of platinum is $1,157.00, for palladium $780.00, for gold $1221.20, for silver $17.43, and for copper $0.1986. Copper troy ounce coins sell for from $1 to $2 each, so they are a poor investment, other than for their collection value. Copper bars are a better investment, but not as compared to other metals. Platinum and palladium are precious metals, but they do not carry the general appeal of gold and silver. People may have some sense of the value of gold, or silver, but few of them will know the value of the other metals.

Gold is the standard among people who invest in precious metals, but silver is the poor man's gold. Historically, silver has outperformed gold as an investment over time. For storage purposes, gold is attractive, because a high dollar value of gold takes little space, as compared to silver. On the other hand, a person can invest in silver with far less cash outlay, and build wealth over time, realistically.

For the person just starting out, with little money, silver is the natural choice. My personal investment policy is diversification. Once I accumulated a substantial amount of silver, I wanted to bring some balance to my holdings by adding some gold. I still buy and hold more silver than gold, but the addition of gold has proven to be a good investment. The value of investment grade coins, whether gold or silver, is driven by demand from collectors. Collector demand tends to keep their value high, even when there is a drop in spot.

The complication the investor faces is that not all silver is the same, and not all gold is the same. There is risk involved in any investment. This is equally true for investors in precious metals. Silver and gold can be purchased as scrap, in jewelry, as bars, in rounds, and as coins. These are offered by weight, or denomination, and each may vary in purity. Smaller weights and denominations usually carry a higher premium than full ounces, or multiple ounces. A 90% pure coin that weighs one troy ounce will not contain as much gold or silver as a coin the same size that is .9999 pure. Even though the 90% coin has less gold or silver content, it may carry a higher premium, and be worth more, and hold its value better, if it is a collectable coin.

Generally speaking, the higher the premium on a product, the greater the risk incurred by the investor, because he or she pays more for a product than the value of the silver or gold it contains. On the other hand, the higher priced product is a better investment, if its collectability value increases over time. A modern .9999 one-ounce gold coin in perfect condition, will sell for less than a hundred year old double eagle, which contains .9675 troy ounces of gold, when it is in circulated condition. An American silver dollar contains .77 troy ounces of silver; where as an American silver eagle contains a full troy ounce. The silver dollar sells for more, even when it is heavily worn. If it is a rare coin of low mintage and in uncirculated condition, its value can skyrocket. As more people become collectors, they put upward pressure on the price, because there is a fixed supply with greater demand.

The lowest premium products usually come in the form of bars or rounds. Governments issue coins, independent businesses mint bars and rounds. Most of the time, government issued coins are artfully designed, and have a higher collectability value. The governments add a premium to their distributors to cover costs, which the sellers pass on to their buyers. Sellers add an additional premium to insure a profit. This is why a person who buys a Silver

Eagle should expect to pay anywhere from $2.50 to $3.50 over spot, per troy ounce. The price goes up if the mintage was low or there is a higher demand from collectors. Coins then have a higher potential for rising in value, but the buyer takes a bigger risk at the time of purchase, because the product may or may not increase in value.

Rounds and bars are gaining popularity as collectable items as well. Producers go to great lengths to offer attractive products in a range of weights. In most cases they are not as collectable as coins, but they still have a collectable factor that contributes to total value.

I am a collector by nature, so I enjoy accumulating collectable coins in my holdings. Some of those coins I believe will greatly appreciate in value over time. Some already have. If I had to sell a part of my holdings, for any reason, I would not want to sell the coins with the greatest potential for profit, so I see a need to have some holdings that are more common. I purchase them with less risk, and use them to protect my holdings of the more valuable products. This is another way that diversification of your investments makes sense.

Now that we have focused on silver and gold, we need to take a closer look at some other principles to consider, and the individual products that are available, to help the reader to make an informed decisions as to what to buy.

Intangible Truths that Affect Building Wealth

In order to help the reader understand my philosophy towards savings, I confess to you, without any shame whatsoever, that Jesus Christ is my Lord and Savior. I have come to believe that the Bible is the inspired Word of God. It is the absolute truth, without mixture of error. I try to judge all proclaimed truth by the principles discovered through the contextual interpretation of the Scriptures. Before I loose readers who come from a different faith, or who claim to have no faith at all, please hear me out. I will make it worth your while, and try to explain these principles for building wealth from both a secular worldview, and a biblical worldview.

The Bible has much to say about finances. Jesus told parables about wise investors. Proverbs is full of wisdom on handling money, and there are many examples from the lives of wealthy, and poor, people recorded in the pages of the Bible. There are two important principles, which are in the Bible, that agree with many of the secular books I have read on building wealth. Charity attracts money, and money attracts money.

Because I approach life with a Biblical worldview, I see everything that I have, or hope to have, as a blessing from God. It all belongs to Him, but He blesses me, and my family, out of His grace. Grace means that God blesses my life because of His love, and goodness, not because I deserve it.

Since all that I have comes from God, I am thankful to Him, and desire to please Him in the way that I the use the material possessions that He allows me to have. The Bible teaches that people ought to help the less fortunate, and to invest in God's Kingdom, to advance His purposes, and to win lost souls to saving faith in Jesus Christ. When a person first believes, they are sealed with the Holy Spirit. Charity is a heart attitude that develops, over time, from the presence, and influence, of the Holy Spirit in a person's life.

A part of the practice of Christian faith is the discipline of tithing. Tithing means that you give back to the Lord a tenth of all you receive from Him. At this point, readers who do not come from a biblical worldview, or Christians who have not discovered the joy in tithing, will scratch their heads. Earlier in the book I went to great lengths to point out the need for discipline in a person's finances, and suggested ways that he or she might save on their spending, so that there could be money in their budget to invest. Here I say, give away a tenth of every dollar you get. This is counter intuitive to most people's thinking, but consider what the Bible says in Malachi 3:10.

"Bring the whole tithe into the storehouse, that there may be food in my house. Test me in this, says the Lord Almighty, and see if I will not throw open the floodgates of heaven, and pour out so much blessing that you will not have enough room for it."

When I first started tithing, it didn't make any sense to me. I didn't think I could possibly give that much money to the church, when I was having trouble keeping up with monthly expenses. I have never missed the money I tithed, and God has more than made up for any loss I might have experienced. As I tithed over time, not only was I able to meet my obligations, my overall financial situation begun to improve. These days, I try to give above my tithe, give other offerings, try to be generous with tips, and look for other opportunities to be a blessing to others. We have a saying in my family, "You can't out-give God." Christians don't tithe in order to grow wealthy. They tithe because God commands it, and they want to please Him, and show their gratitude for His blessings. For those readers who remain skeptical, ask anyone you know, who is a sincere Christian, and a faithful tither, and they will tell you how God has taken care of their needs, and blessed their finances.

The Bible also expresses God's desire that people be faithful stewards of all that He brings to our lives. We are to take care of our bodies, our property, and are taught to put our money to work (investing). God promises to bless those who handle their wealth in a responsible way.

I am convinced that these principles, to some degree, work for people who do not have faith as well, because of the frequency with which they are reported in secular books. Charity helps to put personal wealth into proper perspective. It warms a person's heart. A person who is miserly, and consumed entirely with building wealth, may miss out on the more important qualities in life: love, joy, peace, happiness, patience, kindness, goodness, faithfulness, gentleness, self control, and others virtues that fulfill a person.

A person who is happy, and enjoys life, will be able to think more clearly about financial matters. Others will develop a fondness for them, and a positive judgment about their character. Such a person will be received as trustworthy, which may open new doors of opportunity.

As we think about how money attracts money, by putting into practice the principles in this book, the reader learns how to not waist money. He or she also learns the discipline needed to handle wealth responsibly. Over time, investors learn more, and gain new insights. They mature and make wiser decisions when handling their finances. Accumulated wealth will grow over time, as the investor continues to add to his or her holdings, and as those holdings grow in value. Wealth invested attracts more wealth, through interest, maturity, and appreciation.

Accumulated wealth builds confidence. Without the stress of debt, a person is able to focus better. He or she feels better about themselves, and their lives.

These qualities are becoming more and more rare in our culture. Employers look for confident, competent, and trustworthy men and women, because they need people with character to help them in their enterprise. People who possess these qualities have more potential and opportunities than those who do not.

Have a Plan; Work Your Plan; Adjust Your Plan

On rare occasions, money will fall into someone's lap, without that person earning it, but if he or she does not have a financial plan, that money quickly disappears. Taking control of personal finances, and employing sound financial practices, is the only sure way to build wealth.

The average person may dream of a huge windfall, or that they will hit the winning numbers in the lottery, but the reality is that most people have to be patient, and build their wealth over time. If the reader can grasp the simple truth that they are not going to get rich quick through their investments, they will have made an important first step in realizing their financial dreams.

To get from point A to point B, a person has to know where they are, where they are going, and head off in the right direction. If he or she travels to an unfamiliar place, they will have to ask for directions, or use a map, whether electronic, or on paper. In financial planning, a person must realistically know where they are now, and where they want to be in time. Going the distance takes effort, and to get there in the most efficient way possible, requires a plan.

A person who is in deep debt will never accumulate wealth without having a plan to get his or her debt under control. People who have little or no debt are unlikely to build wealth over time, unless they put a workable plan into action. Investors, who are accumulating wealth already, need to have a plan to continue to add to their holdings.

From these three scenarios, the reader can see that each situation may require a different plan. It is also evident that as a person's circumstances and financial standing changes, he or she may need to adjust their plan. Successful investors learn as they go. The knowledge gained helps them to adjust their plan to more efficiently build wealth.

I am a collector. Growing up I collected rocks, fossils, coins, baseball cards, comic books, postcards, stamps, and anything else that might appeal to the collector inside. This is a part of my nature, and has been a determining force in my choice of investments. Others have no such compulsions to drive their investments. They invest to accumulate as much gold or silver as possible, and at the lowest possible price. Which plan is best? What plan is best for you?

Collectors generally spend more money per ounce on silver or gold, and thus take a higher risk than someone who simply hoards a quantity of precious metal. The higher risk items have a higher chance of appreciation over spot, whereas the most common forms of precious metals remain closely tied to their spot value. Each investor has to choose what works best for him or her. Since both avenues will help an investor to build wealth over time, either plan is good. I lean toward collectable coins, but in case you haven't guessed it yet, I have diversified my holdings, so that I have a little of all.

I began by collecting circulated silver coins. Later I purchased uncirculated silver dollars. When those did not increase in value as quickly as I had anticipated, I looked to bullion, and choose series coins, which had a track record of appreciation. Today the items I purchase are based upon availability, and price, at the time I am ready to add to my investments. I make a judgment with each purchase as to how it will affect my portfolio. I am no longer locked in to the collecting mode, but it still informs my higher risk purchases. Today, balance, and diversity, are more important motivations for my purchases. Other investors choose their investments using different criteria.

The new investor must choose what is best for him or her.

What best fits your personality? What would you most like to have in your holdings? What would bring you the most satisfaction? What are your goals? How much money do you have to invest? How much risk are you willing to take? What works for one person, may not work for another. What does work is investing consistently, over time, regardless of the individual investments.

Another question an investor needs to think about is, "When, or how often do I need to invest?" When I first started out, I did not have much money to invest, so I bought small quantities each pay period. As I became more solvent, and had more investment dollars to work with, I would sometimes save my money for a longer period, in order to purchase a particular item I wanted. Now that I have secured a quantity of precious metals, I tend to hold on to my investment dollars until the spot price falls, and then make a larger purchase.

Larger quantities means lower per unit costs. American Silver Eagle coins, purchased from most dealers, come in units, rolls of twenty, multiple rolls, and monster boxes, which contain 500 ounces. The difference between individual coins and quantity purchases can mean a savings of up to two or three dollars per ounce. This potential for savings also applies for gold purchases. If an investor is able to buy ten ounces a week, he, or she, will probably pay a lower price per ounce, if they can save their money for two weeks, and buy a roll of twenty, one-ounce coins. This is, of course, contingent upon what happens to the spot price during that two-week period.

Buy every week, or save for a larger quantity, and a better price. Each investor must choose what will work best for them. Most brokers will work with investors so that they can buy a fixed quantity of silver or gold each month. While convenient, they will add fees. I prefer to make my own purchases, and I enjoy the hunt for the best deals. Others do not have the time, patience, or knowhow for searching, and are willing to pay a little more for the service, and convenience.

Have a plan for adding gold and silver on a regular basis. Discipline yourself to work the plan, but give yourself permission to change your plan when you're situation, or the markets, change. Now that I have a fair quantity of precious metals, I give myself permission to not make any purchases if the spot prices spike higher than what I deem the purchase would be worth. I continue to watch the markets, and when they return to a reasonable level, I start buying again.

Give Yourself a Break

Especially when a person first starts investing, he or she needs to establish the discipline of saving, and to see how small, regular, investments over time, builds personal wealth. Once an investor learns how the precious metals' market works, they begin to realize that the spot price of gold and sliver moves in patterns. Over one period of time the market will be undervalued, and over the next, it will be overvalued. If the price of gold or silver is inflated, there are other places the reader may invest, which will give a greater yield over time. To recommend other investing vehicles is beyond the scope of this book, but there are some personal investments to consider.

The greatest investment most people make in their lifetime is in the purchase of a home. Everyone needs a place to live. Renting is a poor investment with no return. Buying a home allows the individual to deduct interest paid on the mortgage, thus freeing up money for investment. Equity built into the home increases a person's total worth, which plays a factor in his' or hers' credit score. A better credit score reduces interest charges on loans and credit cards, which frees up more money for investment.

When the market is overly inflated, a better investment might be for the homeowner to make needed repairs, which he or she may have been putting off. A few months back my water bill jumped from about $10 to $40 in one month. After a careful search, I found a leak in a water line that I had put in my back yard years earlier. Money that I might have used otherwise on investment, was better used to fix the leak. I used twenty investment dollars, and a couple of hours of my time, to save $30 per month on our water bill.

Dripping faucets are common causes of wasted money. A

leaky roof, if left unattended, can cost thousands of dollars more to repair, than if the problem were addressed sooner. A small area of rot in one part of the house can grow to cause more damage, or introduce mold and mildew into the environment. Weather stripping gets worn, which causes heating and cooling costs to rise.

Vehicles need maintenance in order to run properly, and efficiently. Needed repairs left unattended will result in greater fuel costs, more repairs, and may result in having to purchase a new vehicle prematurely.

I also believe that most people need to keep at least a thousand dollars of liquid assets in reserve for emergencies. That may sound impossible for some people reading this book, but as you build wealth over time, and learn to apply sound financial practices, this goal will not be out of your reach. When the market is overvalued, you may want to set some cash aside, so that you can be better prepared for the unexpected. When you receive an unexpected windfall, and the cost of gold and silver is high, you might be better served to place that money in reserve. You can always invest it when the market improves, or you can save it so that you don't have to cash in your holdings, and loose their earning's potential, because of unforeseen circumstances.

Obtaining all of the money in the world will not insure happiness. It pays for each of us to invest in our relationships, especially with spouses and children. We make investments in our health. We invest in whatever brings quality of life, which is better by far than having extra dollars in savings. A good steward practices financial responsibility, but not at the expense of quality of life.

Where to Store Your Wealth

One of the most attractive aspects of accumulating precious metals is that you can keep it in your possession, and have access to it immediately in a time of need. The downside of owning precious metals is that if people find out you have wealth in your home, and the word circulates, there is a real danger of theft. For this reason, it is wise not to talk about your holdings, or to show them to others, even if you trust them. A slip of the tongue in a social setting could fall on unscrupulous ears, and you could loose all of your savings. Another danger is that your home might fall victim to fire or natural disaster. An investor needs to consider carefully how, and where, they will store, and protect their assets.

Some take the approach of hiding their holdings out in the open. I used to use a big jar to hold circulated silver coins. Later I moved to a cookie tin, then a wooden box. This is when my holdings were modest, but when, over time, they increased, I realized I needed a safer plan to secure my valuables.

If the investor keeps quiet about possessing silver or gold, there is a far less chance that anyone will come looking for it. Anonymity is your first line of defense. I had to consider this truth carefully before writing this book. So if you ask where I keep my holdings these days, I'm not telling.

Sometimes people take advantage of services that store, and guarantee, their holdings. As you might imagine, this is an expensive proposition for the average person who desires to build wealth over time. The downside to this kind of storage is that the investor does not have instant access to their holdings, and these arrangements generally have to be made at the time of purchase. Another safe option is to rent a safety deposit box at your local bank. This is a very good option for most people. The banks charge an annual fee, but the investor has access, to add to their holdings, or remove them, during normal bank hours.

There has been much talk in recent months, that due to a change in the rules, it will be much easier for the government to seize assets stored in banks, in the event of an economic disaster. This will not be a worrisome for an investor who has confidence in the government, the economy, and the banking system, but in light of the volatility in the world, it is an issue to consider.

Safety Deposit Boxes have a set volume. Bigger boxes cost more money. Chances are, the people reading this book will start out accumulating silver. Over time their holdings will not fit into a bank box, but these boxes can hold a lot of gold. One option is to store the less valuable investments, in or around the home, and store the higher value items at the bank.

Personal safes offer good security for holdings. If the reader decides to purchase a safe, it should be fireproof, and bolted to the floor and/or wall. It should also be mounted in some obscure place, not generally seen by visitors. There are many styles and sizes of safes available. People are often surprised at how much gold and silver can be stored in a one to two cubic foot safe. Sometimes people store all of their valuables in a gun safe.

Other possibilities for storing precious metals include to place them in an inconspicuous box, toolbox, or trunk, and stick them in some out of the way corner in the attic, basement, or closet. Some people store their wealth in the crawl space under their house. Others may decide to store them in an outbuilding, or burry their stash in a waterproof container. I do not recommend one option over another. The purpose of this list is to get the reader thinking about where, and how, they will store their wealth, and to caution each investor to not talk to others about their holdings.

Junk Silver Coins

Junk silver is an unfortunate name given to common, circulated, 90% silver coins, which the government stopped producing after 1964. Silver dollars are in a class by themselves, but dimes, quarters, and half dollars, contain .715 ounces of silver, for every dollar of face value. Many books and websites report that this product is the most inexpensive way to buy silver. It can be a good value, and everyone should include some in their holdings, but it is not the least expensive way to build wealth with silver.

As of the date of this writing, the least expensive purchase price of junk silver, that I have been able to find, is $1.69 over spot. Bullion dealers regularly put silver bars and rounds on sell for $.85 to $.89 per ounce over spot. If an investor is simply interested is accumulating silver, why would they pay an extra $.80 per ounce? Another factor to consider is that the weight of silver in circulated coins is calculated by the amount of silver originally needed to produce the coin. When an investor purchases junk silver, some of the promised content has been lost through the normal wear that comes from being in circulation.

I once purchased a roll of fifty Mercury Dimes on ebay. They arrived in a plastic tube designed for dimes. When I compared them to a roll of Roosevelt Dimes, with less wear, the stack was only ¾ as high. Twenty-five percent of the expected silver was missing. If you buy junk silver, you will pay for the silver content that was originally in the coins. When you sell them, the coin dealer will weigh the coins on a scale, and calculate the actual value of the silver content. If you purchased the silver at spot plus $1.69, or more, the dealer is going to offer you spot, on the actual amount of silver you wish to sell. You just lost a substantial portion of your investment.

There are some positive reasons for buying junk silver. These coins are easily recognizable, and the wear on the coins is evidence that they are authentic. Junk silver is still plentiful and is available through most anyone who deals in silver. Although sold for their silver content, they are somewhat collectable because of their age. When purchasing a quantity of junk silver, there is always the possibility that you might find a rare coin of high value. Familiarize yourself with the key dates, and keep an eye out for them.

Should the unthinkable happen, and the economy totally collapses, these silver coins could become the everyday currency of exchange. If I needed to sell off some of my assets, the junk silver would be among the first to go, while other silver products, with greater potential to increase in value, would be kept in reserve. Buying a roll of junk silver coins periodically is a good way to build wealth, but diversity in your holdings is more secure, and gives the highest potential for building wealth over time.

An excellent resource for determining the silver or gold content of common coins may be found at www.coinflation.com. I often refer to this site before purchasing any silver or gold coins. This resource lists circulated gold and sliver coins, according to their denominations, and tells you exactly the value of the content of the precious metal in each coin, based upon the spot value at that time.

In addition to 90% silver coins, the United States issued "war nickels", with a composition that included 35% silver. These were minted from 1942 until 1945 and are an alternative source of collectable silver. Many people include these nickels in their holdings for their historical value.

The US Mint introduced the Kennedy half-dollar in 1964 with 90% silver. Form 1965 though 1970, they were minted with 40%

silver, and may still be found in change from time to time. From 1971 through 1976, certain Eisenhower Dollars contained 40% silver, but these were issued as a collectables only, and would not normally be found in circulation. Certain modern proof coins also contain 90% silver, but these also are special issues designed for coin collectors, and are a high-risk investment.

When any of the above coins are in uncirculated condition, they become more collectable and carry a higher premium. Uncirculated coins will increase in value over time, if the economy remains strong. Uncirculated silver coins, which have been graded, by NGC, or PCGS, carry an extra premium. Each investor has to decide whether or not to include common circulated, or uncirculated coins in their holdings. I have both, and will probably buy more as time passes.

Collectors sometimes invest in coins without precious metal content. Such purchases are highly speculative, especially among coins issued in recent years. I have some collections of coins, just because I am a collector, but for investment purposes, I stick with coins that contain silver or gold.

Coin Collecting

My interests in precious metals began with collecting coins. My interest in building wealth over time caused me to reevaluate how to spend investment dollars. An explanation of the intricacies required for profitable coin collecting is far beyond the scope to this book. This aspect of investing in precious metals is nonetheless important to consider.

Because I am a collector by nature, I find that my desire to fill a slot in my collection, sometimes clouds my judgment, in my overall investment goals. Adding collectable silver or gold coins to a collection does increase holdings, but the investor must exercise discipline in order to make the best use of his or her investment dollars.

Coin collecting is high-risk investment. Opportunities for investment must be challenged with careful study. The coins that have the potential to increase in value over time have lower mintages, and thus a rarity in the collecting world. People, who have all but the most rare coin in a collection of quarters, are tempted to pay an exorbitant amount of money to have their collection completed. That quarter has value to that person, but he or she may never be able to realize a profit, rather than a loss, on their investment.

The condition of the coin, and whether or not it has been professionally graded, also affects the coin's value. I have many collectable coins in my possession. Some of them I feel certain will appreciate over time. I have purchased some collectable coins at a real bargain, but I paid too much for others. I have some collectable coins that are extremely rare, and have a high fair market value, but they might be hard to sell, and to turn a profit, because there are few collectors who invest in that particular series of coins.

My advice for the beginning investor is to steer clear of coin collecting, at least in the beginning. You already have enough to learn, and to put into practice, without having to take on the added learning curve that comes with coin collecting. There is potential for solid gains, but the risk is high. Focus on your plan to build wealth over time. Accumulate some holdings. If you have an interest in coin collecting, then do your homework, and understand the risks, before you use your investment dollars on rare coins. I may very well purchase more rare coins in the future, but I will be buying as an investor, not a collector.

The American Silver Eagle

Many consider the Silver Eagle to be the most beautiful coin in production. It is one troy ounce of pure silver bullion, produced by the United States government, and enjoys great popularity among collectors, as well as investors. At the time of this writing, the best price I could find on the Eagle is $2.59 over spot, in quantities of 500 or more, and about a dollar more per ounce in single unit quantities.

This is a higher premium than what the investor finds for silver rounds, or bars, but their acceptance in the silver community makes Silver Eagles an excellent coin to add to investor's holdings. The American Silver Eagle is the official bullion coin of the United States Mint. It is available in a proof version at a higher premium. Proofs are made especially for collectors, are more difficult to manufacture, and are produced in much lower quantities. The design for the coin was taken from the popular Walking Liberty half-dollar, which was produced from 1916 through 1947.

The coin was first minted in 1986, and is still in production, as of the date of this writing. Since each coin displays the year it was minted, and because the government produces special eagles, and uses different mint locations, these coins have become very collectable. At first, old school coin collectors, and dealers, scoffed at the idea of a bullion coin increasing in value over time, above spot, but they have been proven wrong, as collectors speculate that buying eagles today, will produce good profits in the future.

Because of the excitement over these coins, dealers often purchase hundreds of new coins and send the best off for professional grading by NGC or PCGS. A coin graded as MS69, near perfect, commands a high premium. A coin that receives a grade of MS70, a perfect coin, may command an almost ridiculous premium. Graded proof coins go for even more. As an investor in precious metals, each person has to set their priorities, as to what investment to make. Anyone who invests in collectable silver bullion should do careful research before spending his or her investment dollars.

Expect to spend at least $35 over spot for the most recent year's graded coin. That represents a big risk, but the market supports these prices. People are willing to pay this much, and more, because they believe the value of these coins will increase over time. Some of these coins carry a premium of a thousand dollars or more over spot. That's too rich for my blood, and is not in keeping with my financial goals.

I am more skeptical, as to their long-term investment possibilities. I do have some graded Eagles, as well as some rolls in my stash, but there comes a point when I feel that the premium is too much for a modern coin. From a practical standpoint I have to decide which best meets my financial goals; a graded bullion coin that is a few years old, and hypothetically coasts $400, or a whole roll of twenty silver eagles from the current year, that costs about the same amount.

The bulk of the bullion coins produced in a given year are in the millions or tens of millions. Most of the specially minted eagles are produced with a mintage of around a quarter of a million. These are by no means rare coins, but investors with Eagle fever treat them as such. If you want to be a collector, by all means, the American Silver Eagle is a very collectable coin, but if you want to build wealth over time, don't get too carried away with specialty Eagles.

Everyone who wants to accumulate silver should invest in some raw silver eagles. They are a low risk investment when purchased by the role of twenty. They are very affordable when purchased individually, even if you have to pay a littler higher premium than with silver bars or rounds. Again, diversity is key in a wise investment strategy.

As with other silver and gold products, quantity purchases can yield significant savings per ounce. An investor can save a dollar or more per ounce if they purchase Silver Eagles in Monster boxes, which contain 500 ounces. Such quantities are out of my reach, and I suspect for most of the readers of this book as well. But what if you could have the full discount; no matter what quantity you buy?

The United States Mint sells specially minted products for collectors, directly to the public, but does not sell common Silver Eagles to individuals. Bullion companies purchase mass quantities of Silver Eagles, and they distribute to other traders and/or individuals. Sometimes bullion companies will put their silver products on sale to move stock, or to attract new business. It is not uncommon for them to offer the 500-lot price on any quantity purchased. To take advantage of the discount, you have to watch their web pages for weekly specials. Others make these offers, periodically, on ebay. Once you become an established buyer, many will notify you of their new specials via email.

The reader can find these ebay offers, periodically, buy refining their ebay search, and limit it to "Buy It Now", and "Lowest price plus shipping." If he or she sets the lower price limit to just below spot, it will get rid of the hundreds of unwanted auctions. Often the investor will search and find a roll, or individual coin, offered at the 500 level discount purchase price. This tip alone can make the purchase of this book a great investment.

America the Beautiful Coins

These bullion coins have been produced since 2010, and commemorate our nation's national parks. Each coin weighs five troy ounces, so expect to pay at least five times the price of a silver eagle. In quantities of 100, they cost about $3 over spot per ounce ($15 per coin), for the ones currently in production. One at a time, expect to pay between $4 and $5 over spot, per ounce. If you decide to catch up and collect them all, you will have to pay extremely high premiums on some of these coins.

This series was highly anticipated by collectors. The United States Mint had some problems with its production, according to the specifications passed by congress. When they finally became available, buyers quickly swooped them up. They are somewhat more rare, because they have a much lower mintage than most Silver Eagles. To date, on the low side, there were only 20,000 of the Hawaii's Volcano National Park coins minted, and on the high side, 126,700 of the Montana's Glacier National Park coins.

These coins look like a Washington quarter on the face, only they are three inches in diameter. There will be 56 total coin designs in the series. Congress directed the mint to produce the series from 2010 through 2021. On the opposite side of the face, each coin has a detailed depiction of the national park it commemorates. These factors make the coins very collectable, and are the reason for their popularity.

America the Beautiful coins are a high-risk investment. Right now their popularity keeps their costs high, and they are likely to increase in value over time, because of the number of people who collect them. If you go online, at the time of this writing, and purchase an ungraded 2012 Denali Alaska coin for $250 to $300, you will still wind up with only five ounces of silver, worth about

$100. A collector will pay a much higher price for one of these that have been graded by NGC or PCGS, and placed in one of their protective plastic cases. The potential for graded coins to rise in value is greater than the potential of a raw coin. Each investor has to determine their investment goals, and the risks they are willing to take.

If in twenty years, that coin rises in value to $1000 in the collector's market, it might be harder to turn it into cash, than a product that is more closely tied to the spot market. There certainly is no guarantee that coin will produce that kind of return. If the economy fails, there is a good chance that the coin would be no more valuable than a common five-ounce lot of silver. The risk one is willing to assume is left to the judgment the investor.

I have toyed with the idea of putting some of these coins in my holdings, but so far I have resisted the urge. Right now, I believe there is better value elsewhere, that is more in keeping with my personal investment goals.

Silver Rounds

Silver rounds are similar to silver coins, but they are not manufactured by government entities. Producers of gold and silver sell their products to many different buyers, governments included. Sometimes they set up their own mints, or sell to companies, who resell the metal to individuals, in the form of bars or rounds. Silver rounds are a popular product among investors to increase their holdings.

Silver rounds are a low risk investment, with their purchase price tied closely to spot. They come in a variety of designs, which make them somewhat collectable, but generally the investor does not expect them to appreciate over time, above the value of the silver content.

One troy ounce of silver in a round is the same content as a troy ounce contained in a Silver Eagle, but the round has a lower premium over spot. Silver rounds may be purchased in fractions of an ounce, but will carry a higher premium per ounce. A few companies offer rounds that contain more than a troy ounce, but one ounce is the standard unit of sale.

On almost any day, I can find silver rounds on sale at a lower cost than junk silver. Bullion companies often have them for sale for $.75 or $.80 less than an ounce equivalent of junk silver, and they are pristine. The buyer receives a full ounce, not a bag of worn coins.

Silver rounds are the approximate size of one-ounce coins. They may be purchased individually, in rolls, or in monster boxes of 500, just like Silver Eagles. Their variety makes them collectable, but the investor should think of them as stable. Accept for a small rise, expect that they will have about the same purchasing power in ten years as they had the day they were purchased. They may be worth more dollars, if the value of the dollar falls dramatically, but they will buy the same amount of products, or slightly more.

When an investor moves into the area of silver rounds, he or she needs to be aware of the possibility of counterfeit bullion. To buy with confidence, the investor purchases from reputable dealers. Buying on ebay should not be a problem, so long as the seller offers the same products that are available from the billion dealers.

While more of a problem with silver bars, ebay buyers, especially, must be aware that sometimes a silver or gold product will actually be plated, rather than solid metal. If a deal looks too good to be true, it probably is. Read the fine print. I have seen many misleading auctions worded to take advantage of innocent, prospective buyers. Even if offerings are legitimate, read the fine print to make sure there are no hidden fees, taxes withheld, or exorbitant shipping charges. Look for an indication of silver content on the round itself. It should say .9999 pure. If it does not, do some more research before spending your investment dollars.

Because of the collector in me, I do not have a lot of silver rounds, but as you might have guessed by now, I have some. In the case of a collapsed economy, I believe any given ounce of silver will have about the same value, whether it is a collectable coin or not. The hundred-dollar graded, Silver Eagle will have the same purchasing power as the $17 silver round. If I have to dip into my holdings, I want to preserve the coins that may regain their value with the recovery of the economy. Silver rounds are a hedge of protection, and bring balance to the overall investments. They are also the least expensive way for the average person to acquire silver, and thus an investment worth considering.

Silver Bars

Silver bars are very much like silver rounds. Governments do not mint them. Private companies produce them to be offered to the general public. When purchasing silver bars, make sure they indicate that they are .9999 pure silver, and not plated. Many sellers on ebay offer "art bars", which have no intrinsic value at all. By the ounce, they often sell for about the same as a solid silver product. Stay away from them. Read carefully before you buy. Search the Internet, and the bullion companies, so that you know for sure what you are buying.

Bars are attractive to the investor because of their stacking ability. They are usually purchased in weights higher than rounds or coins, and thus may have a smaller premium per ounce. Stackable silver products take up less room in a safe or safety deposit box. For the most part, the investor should not consider a bar as anything more than a simple bullion purchase, with little opportunity to increase in value, over time, above the spot value.

Some bars are collectable, in the same sense that rounds are collectable. There are fewer people who collect these than those who collect coins, so it is hard to predict if the most popular or collectable bars will be able to hold any significant value over spot.

Bars are available in fractions of an ounce, but come with a higher premium per ounce. The troy ounce is the standard unit for bullion, but bars become attractive to the investor who wants to hold large quantities of silver, in the smallest space possible. Bars come in weights of one ounce, two ounces, three ounces, five ounces, ten ounces, twenty-five ounces, one hundred ounces, and more. They also come in practical metric sizes form five grams to a kilogram, and more. Which size is the best?

If a person is going to invest in bars, the ten-ounce size is the most attractive way to go, in my opinion. Most people will begin to invest in one-ounce coins and rounds, so there is no need to supplement their holdings with one-ounce bars, unless they are able to purchase them at a really low price. At the time of this writing, in round figures, ten ounces of silver is worth about $200. One ounce of silver is a relatively easy purchase for most people. $200 may hurt a little, but it is not totally out of reach for most investors. One hundred ounces costs $2000, and is not as liquid; it is harder to convert to cash, and to find someone who wants a hundred ounce bar.

Ten, ten-ounce bars, will stack in the same space as a one hundred ounce bar. The investment will be approximately the same, but naturally dividable. Many investors simply stack. They are not interested in coins that may or may not increase in value. Most of these stackers focus on the ten-ounce bar. It is a reasonable amount of money to invest, and over time, they add to their holdings, ten ounces at a time. It's a good plan for building wealth over time. Each investor has to decide what works best for him or her.

Silver Dollars

Early in my investment days, I went to a local bullion broker and told him I would like to invest in a roll of silver dollars. I was surprised, when my order arrived several weeks later, to find he ordered a roll of Silver Eagles. Silver Eagles do carry a token face value of $1, but this chapter deals with the silver coins that were in circulation, and carry a one-dollar face value. These coins are not considered as bullion, and were minted by the United States government prior to 1935.

Silver dollars come in many varieties, but for the beginning and seasoned investor alike, Morgan Dollars and Peace Dollars are prime investment choices. Theses dollars are very collectable because of their age. Before investing in silver dollars, do some research. I suggest you visit www.numismedia.com where you can find a FMV (Fair Market Value) price guide, for not only silver dollars, but for all properly graded United States rare coins.

Silver dollars are not purchased strictly for the silver content, but for their rarity, condition, and collectability. Mintages by year and mintmark are one indicator that determines the dollar's worth, but the US government collected and melted down many of these dollars for their silver content. Value then becomes a function of the number of dollars collectors and dealers determine might be left.

The Morgan Dollar, named after its designer, was minted from 1878 through 1904, with a special production in 1921. The most common, worn, or damaged, dates sell for about one and a half times the spot price for an ounce of silver (remember that a silver dollar is a 90% silver coin and contains less than an ounce of pure silver). As quality and rarity goes up, so does the premium one has to pay. The most rare of the coins in the series is the

1893S. It currently carries a fair marked value of $2,100 in G4 (good) condition. At MS60, the lowest rated condition of the uncirculated coins, its fair market value is set at $115,630. At MS67, the 93S is valued at $981,250.

Probably, no one reading this book will ever have to worry about investing in an 1893S silver dollar, but I use this as an example of how the value of these coins can change according to their condition. For investment purposes, the collector/investor should consider purchasing graded coins, but as with bullion coins, they come with a higher premium. If you buy a PCGS or NGC graded silver dollar, you will have confidence that what you purchase is authentic, and the grade given for the coin is accurate. Should you ever want to sell it, the buyer will share in that confidence.

Beginning in 1921, the US government changed the design of the silver dollar to the Peace dollar. These were not produced after 1928 until 1934, and were discontinued completely after 1935. These follow, in value, the more common Morgan Dollars, with the exception of some key dates: 1921 and 1928. These dollars, for the most part, had a weak strike, so that coins graded at MS64 or higher are extremely valuable to collectors, as compared to the other coins in the series.

I have purchased some of the more common coins, in both of these series, in higher grades, as a part of my precious metals portfolio. They have not performed as well as I anticipated, but they have increased in Fair Market Value, over time. I also have a few rolls of silver dollars. As always, I recommend diversification. On the flip side, when you invest in silver dollars, you are taking a higher risk. Do not take risks until you understand the playing field, and are willing to live with the possibility that you might loose some of your investment.

Other Silver Bullion Coins

Remember that bullion coins that are issued by governments, are distinct from other bullion products, and carry a higher premium. Governments often mint commemorative coins to honor a person, event, or a place. These coins are attractive to specialized collectors, but I steer away from investing in them, unless I can purchase them at, or near, spot.

I have in the past purchased silver coins that were in circulation in other countries, but these are not as recognizable, or collectable, here in the United States. For the most part you will have more security in your holdings, if you invest in silver products produced at home.

Along the way, however, I began to observe that some one-ounce bullion coins, from other countries, carried a higher premium, and seemed to increase more in value, over time, as compared to the Silver Eagle. After researching carefully, I began to add some of these to my holdings.

The Canadian Silver Maple, and the Austrian Philharmonics coins are one ounce of .9999% silver, which can sometimes be purchased below the cost of a Silver Eagle, from bullion dealers, but when sold individually on ebay, they often command a higher premium. These coins are worth your consideration as an alternative, and a supplement to the Silver Eagle.

The Canadian government also produces special wildlife series coins that are extremely popular among collectors, grow in value year to year, but are competitively priced in the year they are minted. The British Silver Britannia is normally priced a little higher than the Silver Eagle. It is another beautiful coin, and highly collectable. As such, its value also tends to grow more rapidly than an ungraded Silver Eagle. Great Brittan, as well as many other mints, produce coins of the Lunar Year Series. While the Lunar coins are more specialized, and carry a higher premium, they are quite popular and increase in value quickly, among collectors.

The Armenian Silver Noah's Ark Coin is growing in popularity and is available in denominations from ¼ ounce to one kilogram. On the subject of the weight of the coin being more or less than one ounce, the investor who is first starting out should probably stick with one-ounce coins. The fractional coins are sometimes produced in fewer quantities, but the premium per ounce is significantly higher than one-ounce coins. The coins heavier than one ounce may be more difficult to turn, should you need to sell. Once you accumulate a quantity of one-ounce bullion coins, you may want to branch out into these other areas.

The coins, other than the Silver Eagle, that have most captured my investment dollars, are products that come from the Perth Mint in Australia. These beautiful and highly prized bullion coins come from the mint enclosed by a plastic capsule. They can be purchased for just a little more than a Silver Eagle, in the current year, but the collectable aspect of their value generally causes them to rise in value more quickly than the American equivalent.

Australia produces a Lunar Series, Koala Series, Kookaburra Series, and a Wildlife Series. In the one-ounce coin, the Lunar Series seems overpriced to me, although they increase in value quickly. The Wildlife Series is relatively new, and I do not have a sense of what kind of track record it will have. The Koala and Kookaburra coins, however, have a proven track record and would be worthy of consideration.

The Australian coins also come in fractional denominations, as well as 10 oz. and 1 kilo coins. A few years ago I began to put away a few of the 10-ounce coins because of the tremendous increase in the fair market value of the coins, over time. These would be some of the last coins I would consider selling.

The Mexican Silver Libertad generally has a lower mintage, and is widely popular among collectors in the United States. It has a proven track record of appreciation. Even though Mexico is our next-door neighbor, only a small percentage of their bullion winds up in the United States. Only recently I added a one-kilo Libertad to my holdings, because I was able to acquire it at a $300 discount over the next lowest availability. The extremely low mintage of this coin made it very attractive, so I assumed a much higher risk, and paid a much higher premium, speculating that it would increase in value over time. I would not have made this purchase if I had not already accumulated a reasonable quantity of base silver. I am always looking for value, and savings, on a purchase, in order to give diversity to my holdings.

The Midas Touch

From earliest historical records, gold has been a preferred standard of exchange. People's and nation's wealth is often measured by how much gold they have in reserve. Gold is expensive as compared to silver, and is probably not a person's first choice for investment, if they have limited means. As a person gets out of debt, and puts into practice solid financial practices, a time will come when he or she may want to add some gold to their portfolio.

At the time of this writing, spot gold is about seventy times the price of spot silver. That means for every ounce of gold a person buys, they could have purchased seventy ounces of silver. Under normal circumstances, the buying power of gold and silver remains the same, or rises slightly over time. An ounce of gold represents a major expenditure, whereas an ounce of silver represents day-to-day expenses. Which is the best to possess? A well-balanced stockpile of both is the probably the best strategy.

I bought a significant amount of silver before I considered owning gold. My first gold purchase was a 1/10 ounce Gold Eagle rated by NGC as MS-70, a perfect coin. I have held this coin for some years. To the best of my memory, I paid $125 for it. Today the same coin can be purchased for around $200. If I sold it today to a dealer, I probably would realize my original purchase price, and perhaps a little more. If I sold it on ebay, there is a pretty good chance I could get something around the $200 mark. Just as coins generally cost more on ebay, they sell for more as well. If I hang on to it, it increases my holdings, and it will probably continue to grow in value over time.

By holding this coin, it increased in value by $75. I expect that the value of the coin will continue to rise over time, but there is always the risk it could drop in value. Modern gold coins tend to be more stable than modern silver coins. Not as many people collect them, because of their cost. A lack of collectability keeps their value closer to spot. On the other hand, I have some Australian silver coins that have increased in value more quickly, each year since I purchased them.

Older coins that were once in circulation do have a high collectability factor, and their prices can rise incredibly high in the more rare dates, especially when they are in uncirculated condition, and graded by NGC, or PCGS. The initial investment for these coins will be out of reach for most people reading this book.

The question then becomes, "Why should I buy gold at all?" Gold may not be the best buy for many people, but I purchase a little gold now and then for diversity, as I build wealth. Remember also that a single ounce of gold takes up 1/70 the space as required by the same dollar investment in silver. This is not a factor for a person just starting out, but over time as he or she accumulates silver, space may become a premium. I haven't sold any of the silver or gold that I have stashed away, but if I had to, a gold coin or two would help me to raise the money I needed quickly, without having to touch my silver investment.

Just as with silver, there are options to consider when a person buys gold.

American Gold Eagles

Like its silver counterpart, the Gold Eagle is a beautiful and highly desirable coin. Unlike its silver counterpart, the Gold Eagle is not .9999 pure. It still contains a full ounce of Gold, but it is 22 karat rather than 24 karat. The coin itself weighs 1.0909 ounces with 3% silver and 5.33% copper. Gold is a soft metal, and the alloy makes it more durable, and gives the coin an overall more lustrous appearance. The Gold Eagle carries a token fifty-dollar face value.

Fewer Gold Eagles are minted than the Silver Eagles, but because of higher costs, they are not as collectable. People who collect them have a more limited market, should they choose to sell. Also, like silver, the higher the quantity purchased, the lower the cost per coin, but the savings is not as much as you might think.

As I write this chapter, I am looking online at one of the bullion brokers I use. If paying cash, a raw, one-ounce Gold Eagle may be purchased for $1,287.67, and spot stands at $1,226.35 per ounce. The highest savings comes with a purchase of twenty or more at a price of $1,278.47. That means a person would have to invest $25,569.40 to save $9.20 per ounce.

I don't know anyone personally, who has that kind of money to invest. I do not often have enough investment dollars to purchase an ounce of gold, and the potential for modern gold bullion to increase in value over spot is limited. The exception to the rule is that some people collect Gold Eagles, which have been graded by NGC, or PCGS, as MS 70, a perfect mint state coin, or PF 70, a perfect proof coin.

Graded bullion coins come with a higher premium than ungraded bullion. The higher premiums bring higher risk, but with better opportunity for the coin to increase in value, above spot, over time. I look at Gold Eagles for stability and diversity in my portfolio, and would not buy graded American Gold Eagles, unless I could find them at, or near, the price of an ungraded coin.

The great news is that sometimes you can find such bargains. Purchasing on ebay requires discipline, to not get caught up in the excitement of an auction, so that you do not pay too much for a product. There are times, however, when someone decides to liquidate his or her holdings, and the savvy buyer may find a bargain. Hypothetically, say a person invested in a graded, one-ounce gold eagle, when the purchase price was $1200. A few years later, the selling price of that one-ounce graded coin moved up to $1500, and the current price of an ungraded ounce was $1400. If the seller wants to turn a quick profit, and liquidate that holding, he or she may offer it at or near the price of a raw (ungraded) coin. Usually these offers will be "buy it now" and they don't last long.

The cost of grading the coin will be around $30. If I am in the market for gold, I search ebay to see if I can find the item I am looking for, and give myself permission to pay up to the going price of a raw coin, plus $30. The added premium will hold to the value of the graded coin, no matter what happens to the spot value, but the potential for increase in value over spot, over time, makes it a better investment.

Many readers of this book will seldom, if ever, invest in one-ounce gold coins, because of the cost. American Gold Eagles are also available in fractional values that put gold more in the reach of the average investor. The US Mint includes, in their selling price to bullion dealers, the costs incurred in the manufacture of the coin, over and above the value of the precious metal the coin contains. The manufacturing cost for a 1/10 ounce coin is about the same as one-ounce coin. For this reason, the smaller denomination coins have a higher premium per ounce than larger denominations. The investor pays less, when he or she buys more.

The tenth ounce, quarter ounce (quarter eagle), and half-ounce (half eagle) coins are more in reach to the investor with limited means, and are a reasonable product to add to his or her holdings. The collectability of these coins will be limited to those that have been graded, and the rules for purchase should follow that of the one-ounce coins. Ungraded coins will have a smaller premium, with little opportunity to increase in value over spot, over time.

Gold is always in demand, and is a low risk investment, when purchased at a fair market price. As with silver bullion products, there are proof versions of these coins that are produced for collectors. These will carry a higher premium. Investors should purchase these graded PF70, and steer clear of coins graded PF69 or lower. The exception is that I have found gold coins for sale, of lower grades, where sellers want to dump them. In such a case you may find a graded coin available for the same as, or less than, a raw coin.

American Gold Buffalo

Most other countries produce their gold bullion coins in .9999 pure (24 karat) gold. Because of investor's outcry for a pure gold coin, congress, on December 22, 2005, passed legislation for the one-ounce American Gold Buffalo bullion coin. The design became available in 2006, and is similar to the iconic Buffalo Nickel, with the profile of an Indian on one side, and a buffalo on the opposing side.

The Gold Buffalo carries the same, or slightly higher, premium as the Gold Eagle. As with other bullion products, it is available in uncirculated and proof condition. The same principles for purchase and investment applies to all; raw coins for building wealth over time, and graded, uncirculated, and proof coins, as a higher risk investment, that may, or may not, increase over spot, over time.

In 2008, and only in that year so far, the mint produced the Gold Buffalo in fractional values. These coins with a token face value of $5, $10, and $25, became very collectable. Collectors demand drove up the value in all denominations. They are hard to find today, unless you are willing to pay a very high premium over spot.

This situation is a learning opportunity for the speculator willing to take a higher risk on any gold or silver investment. Whenever the mint offers a special production of a popular coin, there is a great potential for that coin to increase in value, because of collector demand. The buyer has to be careful though. Hype and excitement over a new issue may drive the price up rapidly, and then drop just as rapidly as the demand decreases. If an investor can get the desired coin early, and pay a reasonable premium, there is a greater chance of a good return on the investment. If he or she waits until the coin has been out for some months, or years, they will most certainly pay more that they could have, or should have.

The mint announces their products in advance, and often posts the mintage limits set by congress. The lower the mintage, the more valuable the coin becomes to collectors. Proposed mintages may not materialize due to a lack of materials, or sluggish sales. Product schedules, along with other valuable information, may be found at the United States Mint web page at www.usmint.gov.

An example of how this information may pay off for an investor may be seen in the example of the coin covered in the next chapter.

First Spouse Half-Ounce Gold Coins

As the name implies, the United States Mint produces these coins, to commemorate the spouses of the Presidents of the United States. These are the government's first ½ ounce coins to be produced in .9999 fine gold, and the first ½ ounce gold commemorative coins. With a token value of $10, they are minted annually, according to a specific schedule set by congress. They are produced in mint state (uncirculated), and proof conditions. Everything about this series defies conventional logic. They are a high-risk investment, with a track record of rapid growth in value.

Beginning in 2007, the mint produced the first coins to commemorate the wives of the first four presidents. Since Thomas Jefferson was unmarried during his office, the corresponding coin bore an image of Lady Liberty, a practice followed for other bachelor presidents. These liberty first spouse coins became a collection within a collection, and generally command a higher premium than the other coins produced in the same year.

The maximum mintage allowed by congress for this release is 20,000 mint state coins, and 20,000 proof coins of each issue. In the first year, the mint produced and sold out all 40,000 (eventually, the final figures were lowered modestly) first spouse coins associated with each of the first four presidents.

In 2008, everything began to unravel. The 20,000 mintage of a mint state coin, or a proof coin, is very low, compared to the tens of millions of other bullion coins produced in other series. Proof coins are generally more valuable, because they are minted specially for collectors, with a mirror-like finish. The mint does not sell as many proofs, because of their higher premiums, and their relative scarcity drives the price up, because of the demand from collectors.

The First Spouse series were collector's coins from their inception, and carried a high premium, as compared to other bullion products. Collectors bought up the proof coins first, leaving the less expensive mint state with lower sells. The consistent lower mintage of the mint state coins made them less expensive to buy, but commanded a higher premium over time, than the proofs.

In 2008, and moving forward, the United States Economy went into recession, and few investors were willing to trust such a high risk investment. The mint was also having trouble getting enough gold to produce the coins, and were faced with other challenges in producing the coins on schedule. In addition, the mint raised the premium, so that the ½ ounce coins were very expensive, as compared to other bullion coins of the same denomination.

The result of the convergence of all of these elements was that the mint sold a little less than twice as many proof coins as mint state coins. This made the mint state coins significantly more rare than the proof coins. In 2008, the mintage figures for the next four First Spouse coins in mint state, dropped to less than 5,000. In 2009, the five coins in the series sold less than 4,000 each, in mint state. In 2010 the trend continued, with only Buchannan's Liberty coming in at a high of 5,162. In 2011, the mintage figures for mint state coins in the series dropped to less than 3,000, and the trend continues as of the date of this writing.

The raw coins have appreciated some in value, but the big gains are for MS70, and PF70, perfect coins. I am fortunate to have been able to add a few of these perfect mint state coins to my holdings. The mint announced the premature ending of the 2009 Julia Tyler coin the day after I purchased one, and the selling price tripled overnight. Since then it has settled to about twice what I paid for the coin, but this demonstrates the tremendous potential of this series.

At this point, the cost of the new raw coins in the series exceeds my investment budget. I will not be adding more, unless my situation changes, so that I have more money to invest. These coins are the highest risk investments that I have made, but so far, have produced the most rapid growth in value. The low mintages make them extremely rare, with a high potential to rise in value. They are some of the most rare coins an investor may readily purchase in todays market, with potential to rise even higher in value over time. A less likely, but possible scenario is that they will fall in value, because of a lack of interest from investors, and collectors, or that their inflated fair market value will make it difficult to find buyers. This is why they are high risk.

On average, a recent release of these coins in MS70 condition will cost between, $200 and $300, over spot. The investor could purchase a significant quantity of other bullion for the cost of the premium. Each investor has to decide how much risk he or she is willing to take, and determine their overall plan for accumulating wealth. Diversification is the author's approach to investing in precious metals. The purchases of First Spouse Gold Coins that I was able to make, have been a positive risk, and are in keeping with my overall plan for diversity in my investments.

United States Commemorative Gold Coins

According to the information posted by the United States Mint at www.usmint.gov ,

"Congress authorizes commemorative coins that celebrate and honor American people, places, events, and institutions. Although these coins are legal tender, they are not minted for general circulation. Each commemorative coin is produced by the United States Mint in limited quantity and is only available for a limited time.

As well as commemorating important aspects of American history and culture, these coins help raise money for important causes. Part of the price of these coins is a surcharge that goes to organizations and projects that benefit the community. For example, surcharges on the U.S. Capitol Visitor Center commemorative coins helped build a new visitor center under the U.S. Capitol's East Plaza.

Since the modern commemorative coin program began in 1982, the United States Mint has raised more than $506,301,189 in surcharges to help build new museums, maintain national monuments like the Vietnam War Memorial, preserve historical sites like George Washington's home, support various Olympic programs, and much more."

As the reader can discern from the above, Gold Commemorative coins carry a higher premium than other gold bullion opportunities. They also have lower mintages, which make them attractive to collectors. As with other modern bullion products, a graded MS70 or PF70 coin is far more collectable than a raw coin.

In my opinion, adding these coins to your holdings is too high a risk, when you look at their overall track record of appreciation. On the other hand, gold is gold, and there are opportunities through bullion dealers, and ebay sellers, from time to time, to buy these products, in raw condition, at a very competitive price, as compared to other gold bullion coins. Sometimes dealers buy these in great quantities, and choose the best of the lot to send off for grading. The coins that were less than perfect, they sometimes want to turn quickly, so that they may invest in other inventory.

If an investor decides to purchase these for sentimental reasons, or to support a worthy cause, that is his or her decision, and the purchase will add value to their overall holdings. In such cases the buyer has conflicting goals, because other purchases, whether high risk, or low risk, offer the likelihood to add an overall greater value to their holdings.

Historic United States Gold Coins

The following quote is from the APMEX web site at www.apmex.com.

"The U.S. Mint issued its first Gold coins in 1795. During the height of the Great Depression in 1933, President Franklin Roosevelt prohibited American citizens from holding monetary Gold including Gold coins. He ordered all Gold U.S. coins to be returned to the U.S. Treasury, where millions were melted into Gold and then cast into Gold bars.

The federal government recalls and melting down of coins made these previously common Gold coins very rare to find. Today, the surviving pre-1933 Gold U.S. coins are fixed at an extremely limited supply. This fact has made Pre-1933 Gold coins some of the most desirable rare coins among collectors and investors."

All of the cautions concerning coin collecting, already mentioned in this book, apply with greater force to collecting these historic coins. Most people starting out to build wealth over time with precious metals will not consider, nor would they be able to invest in, these products. At some point however, investors who have the funds, and are willing to take high risks, will turn their attention to historic United States gold coins.

The $20 double eagle is the standard coin that appeals to collectors and investors. Its design changed several times over the years, and some of the dates command a ridiculous investment, out of reach of the average person. The mint also produced eagles at $10 face value, half eagles at $5 face value and quarter eagles at $2.5 face value. More common dates, and lower values may well be in reach of the average investor at some point in time, but those wishing to add these items should proceed with great care, and learn all they can about investing in these products, before spending their investment dollars.

Foreign Gold Bullion Coins

United States Gold bullion coins are more recognizable to people in the U.S., but a troy ounce of bullion from one country contains just as much gold as a troy ounce from another country. The same basic rules apply for these coins, as for those produced in the United States; accept that stateside, there is less of a demand for graded foreign bullion coins. The variety of designs, however, holds a certain appeal to those who have collector's spirits.

I remain open to purchasing foreign bullion, if I can obtain the gold at a lower price. If an investor is thinking about putting their dollars into a gold purchase, he or she should at least take a look at the variety of investments that are available.

Typically Mexican gold bullion coins command a slightly higher premium over spot, but they have not produced an appreciation over time that warrants the extra risk, in my opinion. The collector may want to have gold from different countries, but the investor is looking for the best long-term value.

The Canadian Mint produces gold bullion coins in the same weights as the U.S. mint, but they are sometimes available for a few dollars less than the American Gold Eagle series of coins. Other countries to consider are China, Great Brittan, Austria, Australia, and South Africa. Bullion coins are fundamentally focused on the total content of the precious metal, and their price follows spot + production costs + distribution profit. Competition in the market opens opportunities for investors to stretch their investment dollars, which is a good reason to consider bullion from outside the United States.

European Circulated Gold Coins

Gold coins have been used for exchange since ancient times. Throughout Europe, they have been used for purchases and investments down through history. During the nineteenth and twentieth centuries, sufficient numbers of gold coins were produced so that they remain plentiful, and available, to investors today.

While these coins were minted for circulation and trade, investors today consider them as bullion coins. They have some collecting value, and coins of high grade, or a degree of rarity, do command an additional premium. Their main attraction, to the average investor, is that they may be purchased at a reasonable premium.

At the time of this writing, the dollars that I have ready to invest will not stretch to purchase an ounce of gold in any form. However, I might consider a 1 Ducat Austrian or Dutch coin at $140 to $150. Perhaps I might raise enough for one of the 20 Franc coins, which were minted in several different European countries, for around $240. If I wait until payday, I could buy a British Gold Sovereign at $300, or go ahead and buy a Half Sovereign coin now.

All of these coins are available at a reasonable premium, and offer a competitive alternative to bullion coins. Looking at the price of these coins, as listed by bullion dealers at the moment of this writing, I can purchase a 1/10 ounce raw gold eagle for $140, or a 1 Ducat gold coin that weighs .1106 ounces for thee dollars more. The Ducat yields a little more gold per dollar investment than the eagle. Similar results may be found with other denominations.

At these prices, gold is not out of the reach of the average precious metals investor. Silver is certainly more attractive to the person just starting to build wealth over time, but do not discount the possibility of adding a little gold, over time, to round out you holdings.

Gold Bars

Gold bars are bullion products that closely follow spot. While there are many manufacturers of gold bars, and some carry a higher premium than others, they are not considered a high-risk investment. As with other bullion products, the higher the weight of the gold bar, the better the price per ounce.

Gold bars are generally available in one to ten ounce sizes. It is possible to find bars heavier than this, but most people reading this book will never spend $12,000+ on a ten-ounce bar. Smaller values will be more in reach, and easier to sell.

Gold bars also are available in a range of one gram to one kilogram. Since a kilogram is just over 32 ounces, most people will not ever possess a kilogram bar in their holdings, but a gram bar is very affordable, although it comes with a high premium per ounce.

I do not posses, or plan to purchase any gold bars for my holdings. I am much more confortable with gold bullion coins, circulated gold coins, and silver products, as I believe they will equal or surpass the relative value of bars, over time.

The Beginning

I pray that the readers of this book will not view this chapter as the conclusion, but as the beginning of a new direction in life. The principles shared, really work, I am living proof, but they take time, patience, and discipline, to deliver the results most people desire.

Remember that this is not a get rich quick scheme, but a plan to help the reader to build wealth, over time. If you want to get out of debt, today is a great day to get started. If you have a little money to invest, start with modest purchases of silver. As you free up more cash, by eliminating monthly bills, and high interest charges, increase your investments.

If some of the principles in this book have inspired you, continue your pursuit of knowledge concerning building wealth and financial security. Please do not make this your only goal in life, but it needs to be a priority that informs your day to day decisions.

Building personal wealth is like being self-insured. Regardless of what happens in the economy, the investor in precious metals has a solid financial base upon which to stand. As a pastor, and a counselor, I understand the stress and hardships that money problems bring to relationships, and how devastating it can be to families. It doesn't have to be that way. There is a way out, but you have to want it, and you have to pursue it.

On the other hand, all the money in the world cannot bring love and happiness to a person's life. There is so much more to consider, that has greater value, and brings deeper meaning and purpose. In my own search for meaning, I found all that I was looking for, in a personal faith relationship with Jesus Christ.

When a person confesses and turns away from the sin, and he or she accepts Jesus Christ into their hearts as Savior and Lord,

God indwells the believer with His Holy Spirit. God's personal presence changes a person, and sets them apart from the rest of the world.

Through the Holy Spirit, God comforts, and protects as He pours His love into a person's heart. People who learn to listen to the Holy Spirit have the very best life possible, under their circumstances.

My prayer for every reader of this book is that you will find true happiness and joy in life. I really do want you to succeed in your financial plan, but even more, I want you to succeed in life, and in the life to come. God has a plan to make that happen. It is available to all people through faith in Jesus Christ.

ABOUT THE AUTHOR

Find other books authored by Greg Robards at:
http://www.amazon.com/Greg-Robards/e/B00GGM7838/ref=ntt_dp_epwbk_0

Follow the author's blog at:
www.gregrobards.com

See author's youtube channel at:
www.youtube.com/channel/UCYlDUuvUaY1IDpUUdl4p6Pg

Greg Robards was born on November 9, 1951 in Louisville, Kentucky. He married Deborah Ufford in 1976 and has two children (Matthew and Elle) and seven grandchildren. God called him into the Gospel ministry on November 8, 1992. He began his Seminary training at New Orleans Baptist Theological Seminary where he earned both the BGS and MDIV with languages degrees. He also earned a Doctor of Ministry Degree from Lake Charles Bible College, a Th.D. from Slidell Baptist Seminary and a Ph.D. in Biblical Studies from Louisiana Baptist University. Rev. Robards served six years as pastor at Pleasant Home Baptist Church in Holt, Florida. In 1999 God called Him to the ministry at Hickory Hammock Baptist Church in Milton, Florida, where he currently serves as Senior Associate Pastor and Church Administrator. Other published works include: Jesus Is God: Commentary on the Deity of Christ in John, Sermons In John (Chapters 1-10), Sermons In John: Chapters 11-21, and Escambia Fill, his first novel. Other interests include Gospel and bluegrass guitar and banjo, gardening, kayak fishing and writing.

Printed in Great Britain
by Amazon

45868901R00053